WHAT ARE FEELINGS?

A Book of Questions & Answers

By Barbara Shook Hazen
Illustrated by Lynn Sweat

Cover by Stuart Trotter

GALLERY BOOKS
An Imprint of W. H. Smith Publishers Inc.
112 Madison Avenue
New York City 10016

What are feelings?

Feelings make you the special person you are. They make your life richer and more interesting. Feelings are what make you happy when a friend comes to play, sad when it's raining and you can't go outside, and proud when you tie your shoes all by yourself.

Do feelings show?

Feelings show in what you say and do. Hugging your family shows that you love them. Waving and shouting "hello" shows you are glad to see a friend. Some feelings show on your face. When you're happy you smile, when you're sad, you may frown. If you're surprised, your eyebrows may raise and your eyes open wide.

Can I feel two ways at the same time?

Yes. It's even possible to feel happy *and* sad at the same time—like when you are happy to be moving to a new house but also sad to be leaving your friends. On the first day of school you may be excited about going back to school and seeing your friends, and also scared about meeting a new teacher and being in a new grade. Can you think of times when you felt two ways at once?

Wow! This is a great present!

Why do I feel happy?

Things that you like make you happy. Eating something yummy, receiving a present, playing with a friend, or visiting your grandparents are all things that might make you happy. Different things make different people happy. Can you think of some things that make you happy?

Why do I feel happy when I make someone else happy?

When you do something that makes someone else happy, you feel good about yourself. If it's someone you care about, it makes you happy when that person is happy.

Why can't I be happy all the time?

Nobody feels happy all the time because things often happen that you don't like. You probably don't feel happy when you are sick, or when a friend moves away, or when you can't have something you want. Happy and unhappy feelings are both parts of life.

Why do I feel sad?

You feel sad when something you don't like happens. You may feel sad when you're not allowed to do something you want to do, when your dog is sick or when you lose a favorite toy.

Poor Spot, I hope you feel better soon.

What can I do for someone who's sad?

Try to find out why the person is sad. Sometimes you can help best just by listening or being there and letting the person know you care.

Why do I feel awful when I do something wrong?

When you do something you know you shouldn't, like eat a cookie before dinner when your mother told you not to, you may feel guilty. Guilty feelings are like a warning signal. Because they make you feel bad, you are less likely to do the wrong thing again.

Why do I feel different ways different days?

Feelings change, just like the weather. Many things combine to make you feel the way you do, from what happened yesterday to something someone said to you. Sometimes even the weather affects how you feel.

Does my body have anything to do with how I feel?

Yes, if you have a cold or a headache, you might feel tired or grumpy. If you had a good night's sleep, you'll probably feel wide awake and full of energy.

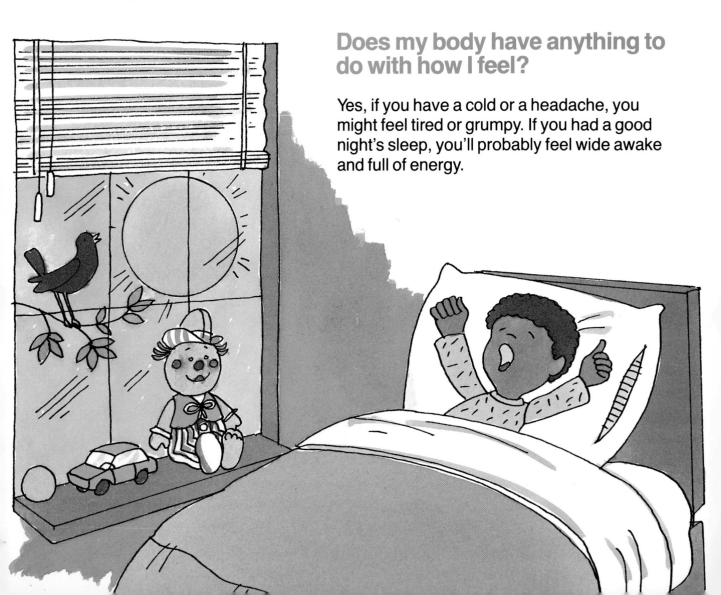

How can I change the way I feel?

Sometimes it's hard. Often you can change the way you feel by thinking differently. You may feel sad when your parents go out and leave you with a babysitter. You'll probably feel better when you remember that this particular babysitter knows how to do magic tricks and tells great bedtime stories. Sometimes a change of activity can change the way you feel. When you act happy, you're more likely to *feel* happy.

Sometimes I get so mad when I can't do something right. What's that feeling called?

It's called frustration. It's the feeling that comes when you just can't do something the way you want to. You try and try to put the last block on the top of your tower but each time it collapses. Finally, you get mad at the blocks and yourself and give up.

What should I do when I feel like this?

Do something else for awhile or ask someone to help you. Don't take out your frustration on anything or anyone, including yourself.

Is it okay if I don't do things right the first time?

Perfectly okay. It's a rare, happy accident when someone does something right the first time. Think about learning to ride a bicycle. It takes a lot of practice. You try and try, and suddenly one day you can do it. What's important is to keep trying until you succeed.

How do I feel when I finish something that was hard to do?

You feel proud of yourself, which is a good, strong feeling. Your feeling of success will make it easier to succeed the next time, too. Your success helps build self-confidence.

What is self-confidence?

Self-confidence is the wonderful feeling of liking and believing in yourself in spite of occasional setbacks or discouraging moments. Sometimes you lose your confidence. When that happens think about all the things you do well and all the difficult things you've learned to do.

Why do I feel I sometimes can't wait another second for something?

You're feeling impatient. You just can't wait anymore. Sometimes a long wait can't be helped, and the best thing to do is to think about something else or do something else to make the time go by faster.

When things don't turn out the way I want I feel terrible. Why?

You're disappointed. It's a special kind of sadness you feel when something doesn't happen the way you expected. Maybe you wanted a bicycle for your birthday, but you got something else instead; or maybe your parents promised to take you to a movie, but when you got there it was sold out.

How do I get over feeling disappointed?

Talk about how you feel, then make the best of it. If you can't go to the movie, maybe you and your parents could do something else together. You'll have a better day if you do something else that's fun instead of sitting around feeling sad.

What is excitement?

It's that happy, eager feeling of looking forward to something that's about to happen. You can feel excited because something you like is going to happen, or because something new is going to happen and you don't know what to expect.

Can excitement be scary sometimes?

Yes, like when you go on a very fast sled ride or hear a spooky ghost story. Being just a little scared is part of being excited.

What should I do when I have scary feelings?

Talk to someone you trust about your feelings. You'll probably be surprised to know that everybody is afraid of something—like big dogs, little bugs, thunderstorms, loud noises or standing on a stage in front of an audience. Never be ashamed of your feelings, even the ones you wish you didn't have.

Why do I get scared in the dark?

Because you can't see in the dark, you start imagining things that aren't there. A curtain fluttering at the window becomes a ghost floating in the air, and a creaky door becomes the step of a monster. Turn on the light and you'll see that everything is just the same as it was before you turned off the light.

How can I help someone who's afraid?

Comfort and try to reassure the person. The fear is very real, even if the monster in the closet isn't.

Why do I sometimes have scary dreams?

Sometimes you have a bad dream about something that really scares you, like witches or thunderstorms. Dreams can also show ordinary things in a mixed up, sometimes frightening way. One thing is sure— what happens in a dream isn't real. Turn on the light, call someone and talk about it, and you'll soon forget the dream.

Mom, it was a huge green monster!

Sometimes I don't like to meet new people. Why do I feel like this?

You're feeling shy. Have you ever gone to a party at a strange house, where you didn't know anyone? Maybe you felt uncertain and scared and didn't want to talk to anyone. Most people feel shy at one time or another. The trick in overcoming shyness is to go ahead, to speak up or to try something new, in spite of your feelings.

Look at all those kids! I don't know anyone except Ellen. Well, here goes . . . Hi, I'm Cindy.

HAPPY BIRTHDAY

How does it feel to be lonely?

You feel lonely when you want to be with someone, but no one's around. Your friend can't come over, your parents are busy, and even the dog doesn't want to play.

How do you stop feeling lonely?

Find someone else to be with, or do something by yourself that you enjoy, like reading a book or playing with your favorite toys.

Why do I feel better when I share my feelings?

It helps you to understand your own feelings to share them with someone. It also gives you the chance to find out how the other person feels. Often, you'll find the other person feels the same way. It's nice to know that you're not alone.

How can I know for sure what someone else is feeling?

Listen to what they say, watch their faces and how they act or, best of all, ask them.

Is it okay when I don't feel the same way everybody else does?

Yes, because everybody responds differently to different things.

Sometimes I feel left out. Why is that such an awful feeling?

Feeling left out is a combination of feeling lonely and unwanted. Perhaps your friends were invited to a party and you weren't. You feel lonely because you've been excluded. It's uncomfortable because everybody likes to be included, but nobody can be all the time.

What can I do when I feel left out?

Think about all the other friends you have. Invite someone else over to play, and try not to let it bother you.

Why do I sometimes feel silly?

Feeling silly is a fun, light-hearted feeling that goes along with being in a good mood. Feeling silly and giggling go together.

Do feelings ever make things happen?

Sometimes, in a roundabout way. The way you feel can influence how you act. Loving feelings, for instance, lead to loving acts. Confident feelings generally lead to trying harder and accomplishing more.

Don't cry Jamie, I'll help you.

I like it when we take walks together, Grandpa.

What is love?

Love is a strong, positive feeling. When you love someone, you want to be close to that person. You care about them, trust them, and want them to be happy.

How does love show?

In many wonderful ways like touching, hugging, giving presents, doing things for the other person and in saying, "I love you." What are a few of the special ways you show love?

Can you love someone and be mad at them at the same time?

Yes. You love your mother, but when she won't let you spend the night at a friend's house, you can be very angry at her, too. When you're angry, that's all you feel at the moment. But when the anger goes away, the love is still there.

What should I do if I'm mad at someone?

Don't keep your anger bottled up inside you. You need to talk to the person and tell them why you're angry. If you're too upset to talk calmly, wait awhile until you've cooled off, then talk.

What should I do when I'm mad at myself?

Forgive yourself and try to do better next time.

How can I feel good about myself?

Think about all the people who love you and all the special things you know how to do. Learn to like and accept yourself, including your feelings.

Why is it important to like myself?

The way you feel about yourself influences the way others feel about you. If you treat yourself with affection and acceptance, most likely, others will treat you the same way.

All these different feelings are very confusing. Will I ever understand them?

Yes. As you grow up you'll become more aware of your feelings and better able to control them. Remember, everyone shares the same kinds of feelings, so don't hide yours. It helps to talk about them. Your feelings are an important part of what makes you a special person.